KAT RENFREW

Manifesting with Moon Magic

A Beginner's Guide to Wishing On the Moon

First published by Nickels for Nana Publishing 2024

First edition

ISBN: 9798337527574

This book was professionally typeset on Reedsy.
Find out more at reedsy.com

Contents

1

Dedication

This book is dedicated to every woman and man searching for their higher self. I see your light and I can't wait to see what you do when you can too.
Love, Kat

2

Preface

I embarked on my moon wishing journey in early 2023, a time when I was seeking purpose and direction. Amidst this search, I stayed open to my inner guidance, trusting the Universe to lead the way. This led me to the local Center for Sound and Ceremony, a place that became a cornerstone in my spiritual path. I am grateful every day for the guidance of the stars that led me there.

At the Center, I was introduced to the ancient art of moon wishing, a practice that has since deeply transformed my life. It has allowed me to align my intentions with my heart's true desires and utilize the moon's energy to bring my deepest wishes to fruition. I hope this guide will inspire you to start your own moon wishing journey, drawing you nearer to your authentic self and the wonders of the cosmos.

3

Unveiling the Magic of Moon Wishes

For as long as humans have gazed up at the night sky, the moon has held a special place in our hearts and minds. A symbol of mystery, transformation, and power, the moon has guided sailors across oceans, marked the passage of time for ancient civilizations, and influenced the ebb and flow of tides. But perhaps its most magical role is the one it plays in our personal lives—as the celestial body that hears our deepest wishes and dreams.

The Ancient Practice of Moon Wishing

Moon wishing is not a new phenomenon. It's a practice as old as time, rooted in the traditions of various cultures around the world. Ancient Egyptians, Greeks, and Native American tribes all revered the moon, recognizing its cycles as a source of energy and transformation. They believed that by aligning their intentions with the phases of the moon, they could harness its power to bring about change in their lives. Whether it was a wish for a bountiful harvest, protection from harm, or the fulfillment of personal desires, the moon was seen as a mystical force capable of manifesting these dreams into reality.

Why Wish on the Moon?

Why do we wish on the moon? What makes this practice so enduring and powerful? The answer lies in the moon's symbolic and energetic qualities. The moon is a celestial mirror, reflecting the light of the sun and, metaphorically, the light of our innermost desires. As it waxes and wanes, the moon's phases offer us a natural rhythm for setting intentions, nurturing our dreams, and releasing what no longer serves us.

- The **New Moon** represents beginnings—a time to plant seeds, set intentions, and make wishes for the future. It's the phase of potential, where anything is possible, and our dreams are fresh and full of promise.
- The **Full Moon**, on the other hand, symbolizes completion and fruition. It's a time to reflect on what has come to pass, to celebrate our achievements, and to release what no longer aligns with our path. Wishing on the full moon is about letting go—whether it's a habit, a fear, or an old dream that no longer resonates with us.

Understanding Lunar Phases

To make the most of moon wishing, it's essential to understand the lunar phases and their unique energies. The moon's cycle, from new moon to full moon and back again, takes about 29.5 days, offering us a monthly opportunity to sync our intentions with the natural world. For the purposes of this book, we will focus on wishing during the New Moon and Full Moon phases, as these are the most potent times for setting and manifesting intentions.

Here's a quick overview of the key phases:

- **New Moon:** A time of new beginnings. Set your intentions and plant the seeds of your desires.
- **Waxing Crescent:** As the moon grows, so does the energy of

your intentions. Focus on nurturing your dreams and taking action.

- **First Quarter:** This is a time of challenge and decision-making. Push through obstacles and stay committed to your goals.
- **Waxing Gibbous:** The moon is nearly full, and so is the energy of your intentions. Fine-tune your wishes and prepare for manifestation.
- **Full Moon:** The culmination of the lunar cycle. Celebrate your successes, release what no longer serves you, and make wishes for closure or transformation.
- **Waning Gibbous:** A time of reflection and gratitude. Acknowledge what has been accomplished and what still needs to be released.
- **Last Quarter:** Another period of challenge, but this time it's about letting go. Release anything that is holding you back.
- **Waning Crescent:** The moon's light fades, signaling a time for rest, reflection, and preparation for the next cycle.

By focusing your wishes on the New Moon and Full Moon phases, you can harness the moon's natural rhythm, enhancing the power and effectiveness of your intentions. These phases provide the perfect balance between setting new goals and releasing what no longer serves you, making them the ideal times for manifesting your desires.

In the following chapters, we'll explore the intricacies of moon wishing, from the language of gratitude and the influence of zodiac signs to the creation of master wishes and the art of manifestation. Whether you're new to this practice or have been moon wishing for years, this guide will help you harness the moon's magic to bring your deepest desires to life. So, let's embark on this lunar journey together and discover the transformative power of wishing on the moon.

4

The Language of Moon Wishes

Wishing on the moon is more than just sending a thought into the universe—it's about crafting your intention with care, choosing your words with purpose, and aligning your desires with the energies that surround you. We'll explore the two key languages that empower your moon wishes: the language of gratitude and the language of the zodiac. By understanding and using these languages, you'll be able to create wishes that resonate deeply with the universe and increase the likelihood of your desires coming to fruition.

The Language of Gratitude

Gratitude is the foundation of any successful moon wish. When you express gratitude, you acknowledge the abundance already present in your life, which opens the door for more to flow in. It's like tuning your frequency to one of receiving, where the universe recognizes your appreciation and responds with even greater gifts.

Why Gratitude Matters

In the practice of moon wishing, gratitude acts as a catalyst, transforming your desires into reality. When you approach your wishes with a grateful heart, you're not just asking for something; you're acknowledging that you are already blessed, and that your wishes are simply an extension of the good that already exists in your life. This positive energy amplifies your intentions and makes them more powerful.

How to Express Gratitude in Your Wishes

When crafting your moon wishes, it's important to weave gratitude into your words. Here are some tips on how to do this:

- **Start with Gratitude:** Begin your wish by thanking the universe or the moon for what you already have. For example, "I am deeply grateful for the love and support in my life, and I intend to invite even more harmony into my relationships."
- **Be Specific:** Clearly say what you are thankful for. The more specific you are, the more genuine your gratitude will feel. For example, "Thank you for the financial stability I have enjoyed this past year."
- **Visualize the Outcome:** As you express gratitude, visualize your wish already coming true. Feel the emotions of having your desire fulfilled and thank the universe as if it's already happened.

Incorporating these elements into your moon wishes will help you connect more deeply with the energies around you, making your wishes more likely to manifest.

The Language of the Zodiac

The moon doesn't just affect the tides; it also interacts with the stars, particularly the zodiac signs, which influence the energy of your wishes. Each zodiac sign carries its own unique traits, strengths, and challenges, and by understanding these, you can tailor your moon wishes to align with the astrological energies at play.

How Zodiac Signs Influence Your Wishes

The zodiac sign the moon is in at the time of your wish can significantly affect the nature of your desires and the energy available to you. For instance, wishing during a moon in Aries may infuse your wishes with boldness and courage, while a moon in Cancer might encourage nurturing and emotional depth.

Below is a brief overview of each zodiac sign and how its energy can shape your moon wishes:

1. **Aries:** Bold, pioneering, and action oriented. Wishes during an Aries moon are perfect for starting new ventures or taking courageous steps forward.
2. **Taurus:** Grounded, patient, and focused on stability. Use the energy of a Taurus moon to wish for material wealth, security, and long-term goals.
3. **Gemini:** Communicative, adaptable, and curious. Wishing under a Gemini moon is ideal for seeking clarity, enhancing communication, and embracing change.

4. **Cancer:** Emotional, nurturing, and protective. A Cancer moon is the best time to wish for matters of the heart, home, and family.
5. **Leo:** Confident, creative, and expressive. Wishes made during a Leo moon should focus on self-expression, leadership, and creative projects.
6. **Virgo:** Practical, analytical, and service-oriented. A Virgo moon is perfect for wishes related to health, organization, and improving daily routines.
7. **Libra:** Balanced, diplomatic, and relationship focused. Use a Libra moon to wish for harmony, love, and balanced partnerships.
8. **Scorpio:** Intense, transformative, and passionate. Wishing under a Scorpio moon is powerful for deep transformations, emotional healing, and uncovering truths.
9. **Sagittarius:** Optimistic, adventurous, and philosophical. A Sagittarius moon is ideal for wishing for growth, travel, and expanding your horizons.
10. **Capricorn:** Ambitious, disciplined, and responsible. Capricorn moon wishes should focus on career, long-term goals, and achieving success.
11. **Aquarius:** Innovative, independent, and humanitarian. Wishing during an Aquarius moon is best for embracing new ideas, fostering community, and seeking freedom.
12. **Pisces:** Compassionate, intuitive, and dreamy. A Pisces moon is the perfect time to wish for spiritual growth, creativity, and deep emotional connections.

Aligning Your Wishes with the Moon's Zodiac

When you know the zodiac sign that the moon is in, you can tailor your wish to resonate with that sign's energy. For example, if you're wishing under a moon in Leo, you might focus on manifesting confidence and leadership skills. Alternatively, if the moon is in Taurus, you could wish for financial stability or a deeper connection to nature.

Here's how you can use this knowledge:

- **Research the Moon's Current Zodiac Sign:** Before making your wish, check which zodiac sign the moon is in. This will give you insight into the type of energy available for your wish.
- **Craft Your Wish Accordingly:** Use the traits of the moon's zodiac sign to shape your wish. For example, if the moon is in Virgo, your wish might be related to improving your health or organizing your life.
- **Be Open to the Moon's Influence:** Sometimes, the moon's energy might guide you toward a wish you hadn't considered. Trust the process and be open to the messages the moon's zodiac sign might be sending you.

By speaking the language of the zodiac, you can align your wishes with the cosmic energies at play, making your intentions more powerful and attuned to the universe.

In this chapter, we've explored the foundational elements that will elevate your moon wishing practice. With a heart full of gratitude and an understanding of the zodiac's influence, you're now ready to craft wishes that are not only powerful but also in harmony with the natural energies of the cosmos. As we move forward, we'll delve deeper into how to use these tools to create master wishes that truly resonate with your soul's desires.

5

Mastering Your Wishes

Now that you understand the language of moon wishes—how to infuse them with gratitude and align them with the zodiac's energy—it's time to take your practice to the next level. In this chapter, we'll explore how to master your wishes, ensuring they are not only aligned with the lunar cycles but also deeply connected to your true desires. This chapter will guide you through the process of identifying what you really want, crafting powerful master wishes, and making the most of your personal moon sign.

Authentic Desires: Discovering What You Really Want

The first step in mastering your wishes is to ensure that they come from a place of authenticity. Often, we think we know what we want, but our desires might be influenced by societal expectations, the opinions of others, or fleeting trends. To create a powerful wish, it's crucial to dig deep and uncover your true desires.

How to Identify Your Authentic Desires

Here are some techniques to help you get in touch with what you really want:

- **Reflect on Your Values:** Take some time to think about what truly matters to you. What are the core values that guide your life? Your wishes should be aligned with these values.
- **Meditate and Listen to Your Intuition:** Spend a few mo-

ments in quiet meditation, asking yourself what you truly desire. Listen to your inner voice—your intuition often knows what you want before you consciously realize it.

- **Journal Your Thoughts:** Write down your dreams, thoughts, and feelings about your current life situation. What is missing? What do you wish to bring into your life? Sometimes, writing can help clarify your desires.
- **Ask Yourself Why:** For every wish you think of, ask yourself why you want it. If the answer feels superficial or unclear, dig deeper until you find the root of your desire.

By identifying your authentic desires, you ensure that your wishes are not only powerful but also meaningful, increasing the likelihood that they will manifest in your life.

Crafting Powerful Master Wishes

Once you've identified your authentic desires, the next step is to craft your master wishes. These are the special wishes that occur when your moon sign matches the sign of the new or full moon when it rises. They are deeply connected to your life's purpose and long-term goals. A master wish is more than just a fleeting desire; it's a statement of intent that resonates with your soul and aligns with the energies of the universe.

Components of a Master Wish

A powerful master wish typically includes the following elements:

1. **Clarity:** Your wish should be clear and specific. Avoid vague or general statements. Instead of saying, "I wish for happiness," be specific about what would make you happy. For example, "I intend to find a fulfilling career that aligns with my passion for helping others."
2. **Positivity:** Frame your wish in a positive manner. Focus on what you want, not what you don't want. For instance, instead of wishing, "I don't want to be stressed," reframe it as, "I intend to strive for peace and calm in my daily life."
3. **Emotion:** Infuse your wish with emotion and believe it. How will you feel when your wish comes true? Adding emotional energy to your wish makes it more potent. For example, "I intend to feel joy and contentment in my relationships."
4. **Gratitude:** As we discussed in Chapter 2, expressing gratitude is essential. Acknowledge the positive aspects of your life and frame your wish as an extension of this abundance.

Examples of Master Wishes

- "I am deeply grateful for the love in my life, and I intend to strengthen my connection with my partner, fostering even more understanding and joy between us."
- "I am thankful for my current financial stability, and I intend to expand my income through a new opportunity that aligns with my passion for creative writing."

- "I appreciate the growth I've experienced in my career, and I intend to take the next step by transitioning into a leadership role that allows me to inspire and uplift others."

Words That Speak to the Universe

The universe responds to words that carry strong intent and clarity. When crafting your master wishes, it's important to use language that resonates with the energies you're trying to attract. Here are some tips for choosing the right words:

- **Use Present Tense:** Phrase your wish as if it's already happening. For example, instead of saying, "I will find peace," say, "I am at peace."
- **Be Affirmative:** Avoid words that imply doubt or uncertainty. Instead of "I hope to find love," say, "I welcome love into my life."
- **Be Precise:** Choose words that exactly describe your desire. Instead of "I want success," be specific about what success means to you, such as "I am thriving in my career as an entrepreneur, with a steady stream of satisfied clients."

Understanding the Daily Moon Zodiac

Each day, the moon moves through different zodiac signs, and each sign brings its own unique energy. Understanding the daily moon zodiac can help you time your wishes for maximum effectiveness.

How the Daily Moon Zodiac Influences Your Wishes

1. **Aries Moon:** Ideal for starting new projects or taking bold actions.
2. **Taurus Moon:** Focus on financial security, comfort, and stability.
3. **Gemini Moon:** Perfect for communication, learning, and adapting to new ideas.
4. **Cancer Moon:** Best for matters related to home, family, and emotional security.
5. **Leo Moon:** Use this energy for creative expression, leadership, and confidence.
6. **Virgo Moon:** Concentrate on health, organization, and service to others.
7. **Libra Moon:** Perfect for balancing relationships, seeking harmony, and justice.
8. **Scorpio Moon:** Focus on transformation, deep emotional work, and uncovering secrets.
9. **Sagittarius Moon:** Ideal for setting intentions around growth, travel, and exploration.
10. **Capricorn Moon:** Best for career goals, long-term planning, and discipline.
11. **Aquarius Moon:** Focus on innovation, independence, and humanitarian efforts.
12. **Pisces Moon:** Perfect for spiritual growth, creativity, and deep emotional connections.

Discovering Your Personal Moon Sign

Your personal moon sign—where the moon was located in the zodiac at the time of your birth—plays a significant role in your emotional life and your natural approach to wishing. Understanding your moon sign can help you align your wishes more closely with your innate tendencies and emotional needs.

How to Find Your Personal Moon Sign

To discover your personal moon sign, you'll need your birth date, time, and location. You can use an online astrology chart calculator to find out where the moon was when you were born.

Using Your Moon Sign in Your Wishes

Once you know your moon sign, you can tailor your wishes to align with your natural emotional tendencies:

1. **Aries Moon:** Your wishes may naturally be bold and focused on personal achievements.
2. **Taurus Moon:** You may find that you wish for stability, comfort, and long-lasting relationships.
3. **Gemini Moon:** Your wishes might center around communication, learning, and flexibility.
4. **Cancer Moon:** You might wish for emotional security, nurturing relationships, and a strong home base.
5. **Leo Moon:** Your wishes could be centered around creativity, self-expression, and leadership.

6. **Virgo Moon:** You may wish for health, organization, and a life of service.
7. **Libra Moon:** Your wishes might focus on balance, harmony, and partnership.
8. **Scorpio Moon:** You could wish for deep emotional connections, transformation, and empowerment.
9. **Sagittarius Moon:** Your wishes may center on growth, adventure, and the pursuit of knowledge.
10. **Capricorn Moon:** You might wish for career success, discipline, and respect.
11. **Aquarius Moon:** Your wishes could focus on innovation, independence, and humanitarian efforts.
12. **Pisces Moon:** Your wishes may center around spiritual growth, creativity, and compassion.

Aligning Your Wishes with Your Personal Moon Sign

When making your moon wishes, consider both the current moon sign and your personal moon sign. By aligning your wishes with these energies, you can enhance the power of your intentions. For example, if the current moon is in Cancer and your personal moon sign is Pisces, you might wish for emotional healing or a deeper spiritual connection, as both signs share a focus on emotional depth and intuition.

Taking Advantage of the Full and New Moon in Your Personal Moon Sign

When the full or new moon falls in your personal moon sign, it's a powerful time for setting intentions or releasing what no longer serves you. These are the moments when your emotional energy is most in sync with the moon, making your wishes especially potent.

- **New Moon in Your Personal Moon Sign:** Set new intentions that align with your emotional needs and long-term goals.
- **Full Moon in Your Personal Moon Sign:** Focus on releasing old patterns, healing emotional wounds, and celebrating your growth.

Start Writing Your Master Wishes

Now that you have an idea about what a moon wish is, it's time to start writing. Whether the full or new moon is in the same sign as your personal moon sign or not, you can still make powerful wishes. Here's a step-by-step guide to help you craft your master wishes and regular wishes:

- **Find a comfortable** space where you can focus without distractions. This could be a cozy corner of your home, a peaceful spot in nature, or any place where you feel at ease.
- **Set the mood** by creating an atmosphere that supports your intention-setting. Light candles, play soft music, or use essential oils to enhance the ambiance. This helps you get into the right mindset for making your wishes.
- **Write your wishes.** For regular wishes, write them within

24 hours of the full or new moon, using the language and qualities associated with the zodiac sign the moon is in. For example, if the moon is in Taurus, focus on stability, comfort, and abundance. For master wishes, if the full or new moon is in the same sign as your personal moon sign, take advantage of this powerful alignment. Make your biggest wishes! Write your master wishes within 48 hours of the full or new moon, aligning them with your emotional needs and long-term goals.

Use the language of the zodiac to tailor your wishes to the energy of the current moon sign. This enhances the potency of your intentions. For example:

1. **Aries Moon:** Bold, action-oriented wishes.
2. **Taurus Moon:** Wishes for stability and comfort.
3. **Gemini Moon:** Wishes related to communication and learning.
4. **Cancer Moon:** Emotional security and nurturing relationships.
5. **Leo Moon:** Creativity and self-expression.
6. **Virgo Moon:** Health and organization.
7. **Libra Moon:** Balance and harmony.
8. **Scorpio Moon:** Transformation and deep emotional connections.
9. **Sagittarius Moon:** Growth and adventure.
10. **Capricorn Moon:** Career success and discipline.
11. **Aquarius Moon:** Innovation and independence.
12. **Pisces Moon:** Spiritual growth and compassion.

- Make it a ritual by speaking your wishes out loud. Whether you choose to wish alone or with others, vocalizing your wishes to the moon helps send your intentions into the universe. Imagine your words flying up to the moon, carrying your desires with them.
- Feel the emotions associated with your wishes as you write and speak them. Visualize your wishes coming true and experience the joy, peace, or excitement that accompanies their manifestation.
- Trust the process. After making your wishes, trust that the universe is working to bring them to fruition. Stay open to receiving your desires in whatever form they come.

By following these steps, you can create a powerful ritual that aligns your wishes with the lunar energies and enhances their manifestation. Remember, the key is consistency and intention. As you continue on your moon wishing journey, these practices will help you create intentions that resonate deeply with your soul and bring your dreams closer to reality.

6

I've Made My Wish, Now What?

Making your wish is just the beginning. Like planting a seed, your wish needs time, attention, and the right conditions to grow and manifest into reality. In this chapter, we'll explore what happens after you've made your wish, how to stay aligned with your intentions, and the role of intuition and gratitude in the manifestation process.

Whose Wishes Come True? Pie for All!

One of the most beautiful aspects of moon wishing is that it's available to everyone. Just as the moon shines on all of us equally, the universe listens to every wish, regardless of who you are or where you come from. But why do some wishes come true while others seem to fade into the ether?

The answer lies in the energy and intention behind your wish, as well as your ability to align with the flow of the universe. The "Pie for All" concept reminds us that the universe is abundant and there is enough for everyone. Your wish doesn't take away from anyone else's, and their wishes don't diminish yours. When you trust in this abundance, you open yourself up to receive the blessings that are meant for you.

Why Hasn't My Wish Come True? (Hint: Follow Your Intuition.)

It's not uncommon to feel impatient or frustrated if your wish doesn't manifest as quickly as you'd hoped. But just because you don't see immediate results doesn't mean your wish isn't on its way. The universe works in mysterious ways, and sometimes the timing isn't quite right, or there are unseen factors at play.

Common Reasons for Delayed Manifestation

- **Timing:** The universe operates on its own timeline, which may not always align with yours. Trust that your wish will manifest at the perfect time.
- **Alignment:** Sometimes, your wish may require you to make certain changes in your life to align with what you're asking for. This could involve letting go of old habits, embracing new opportunities, or shifting your mindset.
- **Hidden Blocks**: Emotional or mental blocks can sometimes interfere with the manifestation process. If you feel stuck, consider whether there are any fears, doubts, or limiting beliefs that need to be addressed.

The Role of Intuition

Your intuition is a powerful guide in the manifestation process. After making your wish, pay attention to any intuitive nudges or insights that arise. These may come in the form of sudden ideas, dreams, or even feelings that guide you toward actions that will help your wish come true. Trust your inner wisdom and follow these prompts, even if they don't seem directly related to your wish.

Your Wish Comes True, Return the Gratitude

Gratitude is the final and perhaps most important step in the wishing process. When your wish comes true, take time to acknowledge it and express your thanks. Gratitude not only reinforces the positive energy you've already put out into the universe but also keeps the cycle of abundance flowing.

How to Practice Gratitude

Acknowledge Your Wish: When your wish manifests, take a moment to recognize it. This might seem obvious, but it's easy to overlook the small ways in which your wish may come true.

Give Thanks: Express your gratitude in whatever way feels most natural to you. You might say a simple "thank you" to the universe, write in a gratitude journal, or even perform a small ritual to honor the manifestation.

Pay It Forward: Consider sharing your good fortune with others. This could be as simple as helping someone else with their own wishes, or it could involve giving back in a way that aligns with the blessing you've received.

How to Write a Moon Wish for Someone Else

While moon wishing is often a personal practice, you can also use it to send positive energy and intentions to others. Writing a moon wish for someone else is a beautiful way to share the power of the moon's energy and support those you care about.

Steps to Writing a Wish for Someone Else

1. **Focus on Their Highest Good**: When writing a wish for someone else, always keep their highest good in mind. Avoid imposing your own desires or expectations on them. Instead, wish for their happiness, health, or whatever they most need.

2. **Use Positive Language:** Frame your wish in a positive and affirming way. For example, instead of saying, "I wish for them to stop struggling," say, "I intend for them to find peace and ease in their life."

3. **Respect Their Free Will:** Remember that everyone has their own path and free will. Your wish should never try to control or manipulate their choices. Instead, focus on sending them love, support, and positive energy.

4. **Infuse Your Wish with Love:** As you write the wish, imagine filling it with loving energy. You can even visualize the person surrounded by light and receiving your wish with open arms.

Example of a Wish for Someone Else:

"I am grateful for [Name]'s presence in my life, and I intend for them to find the courage and clarity to pursue their dreams with confidence. May they be surrounded by love and support as they navigate their journey, and may they find joy and fulfillment in every step they take. Thank you."

Nurturing Your Wishes: Staying Aligned with Your Intentions

Once you've made your wish, it's important to stay aligned with your intentions. This means continuing to live in a way that supports your wish and keeps you connected to the energy you've put into the universe.

Daily Practices to Support Your Wishes

- **Mindfulness:** Stay present and mindful in your daily life. This helps you remain aware of opportunities or signs that may support your wish.
- **Affirmations**: Use affirmations to keep your mind focused on your wish. Repeat positive statements that reinforce the belief that your wish is coming true.
- **Visualization:** Regularly visualize your wish as if it has already manifested. This keeps your energy aligned with your desired outcome.
- **Self-Care:** Take care of yourself physically, emotionally, and spiritually. When you're in a positive state of well-being, you're more receptive to the energy of the universe.

In this chapter, we've explored what to do after making your wish, from following your intuition to practicing gratitude. Remember, the manifestation process is a journey that requires patience, trust, and alignment with the flow of the universe. By staying connected to your intentions and nurturing your wishes, you can create a life that reflects your deepest desires and brings you closer to your true purpose.

Next, we'll delve into fine-tuning your power wish with tools and techniques like moon water and vision boards, helping you amplify the energy behind your intentions and make your wishes even more potent.

7

Fine-Tuning Your Master Wish

As you've learned throughout this journey, making a wish on the moon is a deeply personal and spiritual practice. But what if you could amplify the power of your wish even further? In this chapter, we'll explore advanced techniques for fine-tuning your master wish, including how to make moon water, create a vision board, and other practices that will help you harness the full potential of your intentions.

How to Make Moon Water

Moon water is a sacred tool used in various spiritual practices to capture the energy of the moon. By collecting and using this water, you can infuse your wishes, rituals, and everyday life with the moon's powerful energy.

What You'll Need:

1. **A Glass Bottle or Mason Jar:** Ensure it's something that can be securely closed with a cork or lid.
2. **Spring Water or Filtered Water:** Use high-quality water to ensure purity.
3. **Cheesecloth or Cork:** To stopper the bottle and protect the water.
4. **Crystals (Optional):** Place crystals next to the bottle, not inside, to avoid contamination.

Steps to Create Moon Water:

- **Choose the Right Moon Phase:** Decide whether you want to make your moon water during the full moon or the new moon, depending on your intention. Full moon water is great for releasing and cleansing, while new moon water is ideal for setting intentions and manifesting new beginnings.

- **Set Your Intention:** Before placing the water outside, hold the bottle or jar in your hands and focus on your intention. Visualize the moon's energy infusing the water with the power to support your wish.
- **Leave It Overnight:** Place the jar or bottle of water in a spot where it can absorb the moonlight. (Even if you can't see the moon, the moon will see your jar or bottle.) Leave it there overnight, allowing the water to be charged with the moon's energy. If you're using crystals, place them next to the bottle to enhance the energy, but avoid putting them directly into the water.
- **Retrieve and Store:** In the morning, retrieve your moon water. You can store it in a cool, dark place, and use it in your rituals, baths, or to water your plants. Whenever you use it, remember the intention you set and the power of the moon that exists within it.

Ways to Use Moon Water:

- Ritual Baths: Add moon water to your bath to cleanse your energy and align with your intentions.
- Anointing: Use moon water to anoint yourself, your tools, or your sacred space, enhancing the power of your wishes.
- Drinking: If you feel drawn to do so, you can drink moon water (make sure it's safe and clean) to internalize the moon's energy and manifest your intentions from within.

Make a Vision Board

A vision board is a powerful tool that helps you visualize your goals and dreams. By creating a physical representation of your wishes, you can keep your intentions at the forefront of your mind and stay motivated to achieve them.

What You'll Need:

- A Board or Large Piece of Paper: This will be the base of your vision board.
- Magazines, Printouts, or Drawings: Gather images, words, and symbols that stand for your wishes and dreams.
- Glue, Scissors, and Markers: To cut out and arrange your images and words on the board.

Steps to Create Your Vision Board:

- **Set Your Intention:** Begin by reflecting on your wishes and what you want to manifest. Think about the feelings, experiences, and outcomes you want.
- **Collect Images and Words:** Look through magazines, online images, or even create your own drawings that resonate with your wishes. Choose visuals that evoke the emotions and energy you want to attract.
- **Arrange and Glue:** Once you've gathered your materials, start arranging them on your board. There's no right or wrong way to do this—just follow your intuition and create a collage that feels meaningful to you.
- **Place Your Vision Board Somewhere Visible:** Keep your vision board in a place where you'll see it daily, like your

bedroom, workspace, or altar. Each time you look at it, you'll reinforce your intentions and stay aligned with your goals.

Using Your Vision Board:

- **Daily Reflection:** Spend a few minutes each day looking at your vision board and reflecting on your goals. Visualize yourself achieving them and feel the emotions that come with success.
- **Affirmations:** As you gaze at your vision board, repeat affirmations that support your wishes. For example, "I am open to receiving abundance in all areas of my life."
- **Revisit and Update:** As your goals evolve, don't hesitate to update your vision board. It's a living, breathing represen-tation of your dreams, so let it grow with you.

Additional Techniques for Enhancing Your Wish Craft

In addition to moon water and vision boards, there are other practices you can incorporate into your wish-making routine to further amplify your intentions.

Crystal Magic

Crystals are known for their unique energies and can be powerful allies in the manifestation process. Different crystals resonate with different intentions, so choose ones that align with your wishes.

- **Amethyst:** For spiritual growth and clarity.
- **Rose Quartz:** For love, compassion, and emotional healing.
- **Citrine:** For abundance, prosperity, and joy.
- **Moonstone:** For intuition, feminine energy, and connection to the moon.

To use crystals in your wish craft, you can meditate with them, place them on your vision board, or even infuse them in your moon water. (**Do not place crystals directly into your moon water.** Place the crystals in close proximity to your bottle, preferably touching the outside of the bottle.)

Affirmations and Mantras

Words have power, and using affirmations or mantras can help you stay focused and aligned with your wishes. Choose phrases that resonate with your intentions and repeat them daily to reinforce your beliefs.

Examples of affirmations:

- "I am worthy of all the good things coming my way."
- "I trust the universe to bring my desires into reality."
- "My wishes are already manifesting, and I am grateful."

Journaling

Keeping a journal dedicated to your moon wishes can be a powerful way to track your progress, reflect on your intentions, and express gratitude. Write about your wishes, the signs you notice, and how you feel as you move closer to manifesting your desires.

Bringing It All Together

Fine-tuning your power wish is about more than just making a wish; it's about fully engaging with the process, aligning your energy with your desires, and using tools that resonate with your unique spiritual practice. Whether you're creating moon water, crafting a vision board, or working with crystals, each of these techniques adds another layer of intention and focus to your wishes.

By incorporating these practices into your moon wishing routine, you'll not only enhance the power of your wishes but also deepen your connection to the moon, the universe, and yourself. Remember, the magic of moon wishing lies in the combination of belief, intention, and action. As you continue on this path, trust that the universe is working in harmony with you to bring your deepest desires to life.

8

Conclusion

As you reach the end of this guide, you've embarked on a journey that connects you with the ancient and mystical practice of moon wishing. Throughout these pages, you've discovered the power of intention, the significance of lunar phases, and the ways to harness the moon's energy to manifest your deepest desires. Now, it's time to reflect on what you've learned and how you can carry these practices forward in your life.

Reflecting on the Journey

The moon has been a source of wonder and inspiration for countless generations. It governs the tides, illuminates the night, and influences our emotions and intuition. By tuning into the moon's cycles, you've opened a doorway to a deeper understanding of yourself and the universe around you.

You've learned that the new moon is a time for planting seeds, setting intentions, and inviting new beginnings. The full moon, on the other hand, is a time of release, completion, and letting go of what no longer serves you. By aligning your wishes with these lunar phases, you can create a powerful flow of energy that supports your goals and dreams.

Carrying the Practice Forward

Now that you're equipped with the knowledge and tools to make moon wishes, the next step is to make this practice a regular part of your life. Whether you choose to make wishes with every new and full moon or simply when you feel called to do so, the key is consistency and intention.

Here are a few ways to continue your moon wishing practice:

1. **Create a Ritual:** Set up a personal ritual that you can perform each month during the new and full moons. This could include lighting candles, meditating, journaling, or making moon water.

2. **Keep a Moon Journal:** Document your dreams, wishes, the lunar phases, and any signs or synchronicity you notice. This will help you track your progress and deepen your connection to the moon.

3. **Stay Open to the Universe:** Trust that the universe is always working in your favor. Sometimes wishes manifest in ways we don't expect, so stay open to receiving your desires in whatever form they come.

4. **Share the Magic:** Consider sharing your moon wishing practice with friends or loved ones. Not only does this spread the magic, but it also strengthens your intentions through collective energy.

A Word on Gratitude

As you continue to make wishes, never forget the importance of gratitude. Expressing thanks, both before and after your wishes come true, is a powerful way to keep the energy flowing. Gratitude is the key that unlocks the door to abundance, and by maintaining an attitude of thankfulness, you align yourself with the flow of positive energy in the universe.

Embrace the Magic

Remember, moon wishing is not just about asking for what

you want; it's about connecting with the natural rhythms of the earth and sky, and aligning yourself with the energies that govern our lives. It's about trusting in the process, believing in your own power, and allowing the magic of the moon to guide you on your journey.

As you step away from this guide and into the world, take with you the knowledge that you are a powerful co-creator of your reality. The moon is your ally, and with each phase, it offers you a new opportunity to manifest your dreams and desires.

May your wishes always be aligned with the highest good and may the light of the moon illuminate your path, guiding you toward your truest and most fulfilling life.

9

References

1. "Moon Phases 2025 – Lunar Calendar for EDT." Timeand-date.com, accessed August 21, 2024, https://www.timeand date.com/moon/phases/usa/new-york?year=2025.

2. "Free Birth Chart Calculator." Astrology.com, accessed August 21, 2024, https://www.astrology.com/birth-chart-calculator.

3. Nick Greene. "Zodiac Signs and the Words That Describe Them." Thoughtco.com, accessed August 21, 2024, https://www.thoughtco.com/zodiac-signs-and-the-word s-that-describe-them-206981.

4. "Thesaurus by Merriam-Webster: Find Synonyms, Similar Words, and Antonyms." Merriam-Webster, accessed August 21, 2024, https://www.merriam-webster.com/thesau rus.

5. "Magic of the Moon: A Guide to Wiccan Moon Magic, Phases, and Ceremonies." Craft of Wicca, accessed August

21, 2024, https://www.craftofwicca.com/magic-of-the-m
oon.

6. "Full Moon and New Moon Rituals—Intention Setting
and Actualization." We'Moon, accessed August 21, 2024,
https://www.wemoon.ws/full-moon-and-new-moon-rit
uals.

7. "Aries Zodiac Sign: Characteristics, Dates, & More." As-
trology.com, accessed August 21, 2024, https://www.astro
logy.com/zodiac-signs/aries.

8. "Aries Sun, Aries Moon, Aries Rising - Meaning." Astrol-
ogy.com, accessed August 21, 2024, https://www.astrolog
y.com/aries-sun-moon-rising.

9. "Aries Words: Unlock Your Inner Power With Aries-
Inspired Vocabulary." TheReadingTub, accessed August
21, 2024, https://www.thereadingtub.com/aries-words.

10. "Taurus Zodiac Sign: Characteristics, Dates, & More."
Astrology.com, accessed August 21, 2024, https://www.
astrology.com/zodiac-signs/taurus.

11. "Taurus Sun, Taurus Moon, Taurus Rising - Meaning."
Astrology.com, accessed August 21, 2024, https://www.
astrology.com/taurus-sun-moon-rising.

12. "Gemini Zodiac Sign: Characteristics, Dates, & More."
Astrology.com, accessed August 21, 2024, https://www.
astrology.com/zodiac-signs/gemini.

13. "The Moon in Gemini Traits & Meaning in Astrology."
Astrology.com, accessed August 21, 2024, https://www.
astrology.com/moon-in-gemini.

14. "Cancer Zodiac Sign: Characteristics, Dates, & More."
Astrology.com, accessed August 21, 2024, https://www.
astrology.com/zodiac-signs/cancer.

15. "The Moon in Cancer Traits & Meaning in Astrology."

Astrology.com, accessed August 21, 2024, https://www.astrology.com/moon-in-cancer.

16. "Leo Zodiac Sign: Characteristics, Dates, & More." Astrology.com, accessed August 21, 2024, https://www.astrology.com/zodiac-signs/leo.

17. "The Moon in Leo Traits & Meaning in Astrology." Astrology.com, accessed August 21, 2024, https://www.astrology.com/moon-in-leo.

18. "Virgo Zodiac Sign: Characteristics, Dates, & More." Astrology.com, accessed August 21, 2024, https://www.astrology.com/zodiac-signs/virgo.

19. "Virgo Moon: Meaning, Traits, Personality." Astrology.com, accessed August 21, 2024, https://www.astrology.com/virgo-moon.

20. "Libra Zodiac Sign: Characteristics, Dates, & More." Astrology.com, accessed August 21, 2024, https://www.astrology.com/zodiac-signs/libra.

21. "The Moon in Libra Traits & Meaning in Astrology." Astrology.com, accessed August 21, 2024, https://www.astrology.com/moon-in-libra.

22. "Scorpio Zodiac Sign: Characteristics, Dates, & More." Astrology.com, accessed August 21, 2024, https://www.astrology.com/zodiac-signs/scorpio.

23. "The Moon in Scorpio Traits & Meaning in Astrology." Astrology.com, accessed August 21, 2024, https://www.astrology.com/moon-in-scorpio.

24. "Sagittarius Zodiac Sign: Characteristics, Dates, & More." Astrology.com, accessed August 21, 2024, https://www.astrology.com/zodiac-signs/sagittarius.

25. "The Moon in Sagittarius Traits & Meaning in Astrology." Astrology.com, accessed August 21, 2024, https://www.ast

rology.com/moon-in-sagittarius.

26. "Capricorn Zodiac Sign: Characteristics, Dates, & More." Astrology.com, accessed August 21, 2024, https://www.ast rology.com/zodiac-signs/capricorn.

27. "The Moon in Capricorn Traits & Meaning in Astrology." Astrology.com, accessed August 21, 2024, https://www.ast rology.com/moon-in-capricorn.

28. "Aquarius Zodiac Sign: Characteristics, Dates, & More." Astrology.com, accessed August 21, 2024, https://www.ast rology.com/zodiac-signs/aquarius.

29. "The Moon in Aquarius Traits & Meaning in Astrology." Astrology.com, accessed August 21, 2024, https://www.ast rology.com/moon-in-aquarius.

30. "Pisces Zodiac Sign: Characteristics, Dates, & More." Astrology.com, accessed August 21, 2024, https://www.astro logy.com/zodiac-signs/pisces.

31. "The Moon in Pisces Traits & Meaning in Astrology." Astrology.com, accessed August 21, 2024, https://www. astrology.com/moon-in-pisces.

32. "How to Make Your Own Moon Water: Origins, Lore, and DIY Ritual." Healthline, accessed August 21, 2024, https://www.healthline.com/health/moon-water.

33. "Ways to Say Thank You." Verywell Mind, accessed August 21, 2024, https://www.verywellmind.com/ways-to-say-t hank-you-8597809.

34. "Ways to Say Thank You for All That You Do." Handwrytten, accessed August 21, 2024, https://www.handwrytten.com/ resources/ways-to-say-thank-you-for-all-that-you-do.

35. "Gratitude." Merriam-Webster, accessed August 21, 2024, https://www.merriam-webster.com/thesaurus/gratitude.

36. "Beyond Thank You: Show Appreciation & Express Grat-

itude in English." English with Kim, accessed August 21, 2024, https://englishwithkim.com/beyond-thank-you-show-appreciation-express-gratitude-english.

37. "Phrases to Express Gratitude in English." Speak Confident English, accessed August 21, 2024, https://www.speakconfidentenglish.com/phrases-to-express-gratitude-in-english.

38. "How to Create an Awesome Vision Board in 8 Simple Steps." Science of People, accessed August 21, 2024, https://www.scienceofpeople.com/vision-board.

39. Moon Spells for Witchcraft: A Guide to Using the Lunar Phases for Magic ..., https://www.magickandwitchcraft.com/post/moon-spells-for-witchcraft-a-guide-to-using-the-lunar-phases-for-magic-and-rituals.

40. Crystal magick for self-discovery, https://crystalclaritygems.com/crystal-magick-for-self-discovery-unveil-your-true-self-with-the-power-of-healing-crystals/.

41. Crystals for Moon Water Magic: A Step-by-Step Guide, https://allthecrystals.com/crystals-for-moon-water/.

42. Moon Rituals: Modern Ways to Harness Lunar Energies, https://www.spiritdelalune.com/lunar/moon-rituals/.

43. Cover image created by Heather Renfrew via Microsoft CoPilot, 8/26/2024

10

About the Author

Kat Renfrew, originally from Mobile, Alabama, relocated to Central New York during her teenage years. She has resided in Pittsburgh, Pennsylvania, where she pursued studies at AIP. In 2007, she served as an action station chef for Levy's at the club level of PNC Park. Following the birth of her child, her family returned to Central New York in 2009. Between 2016 and 2023, she refined her expertise as a machine operator at a factory in Fulton, New York, until a shift in the universe prompted her to seek a new career path. Now self-employed and working towards an NLP life coach certification, she lives on a tranquil street in upstate New York, surrounded by her family, beloved pets, and engaging in hobbies like gardening and knitting.

Kat enjoying herself at Breitbeck Park on Lake Ontario.